First and Last

Teacher's Choice Series

Donna Chicca
Bakersfield, California

Illustrations by
Andrew Geeson

Dominie Press, Inc.

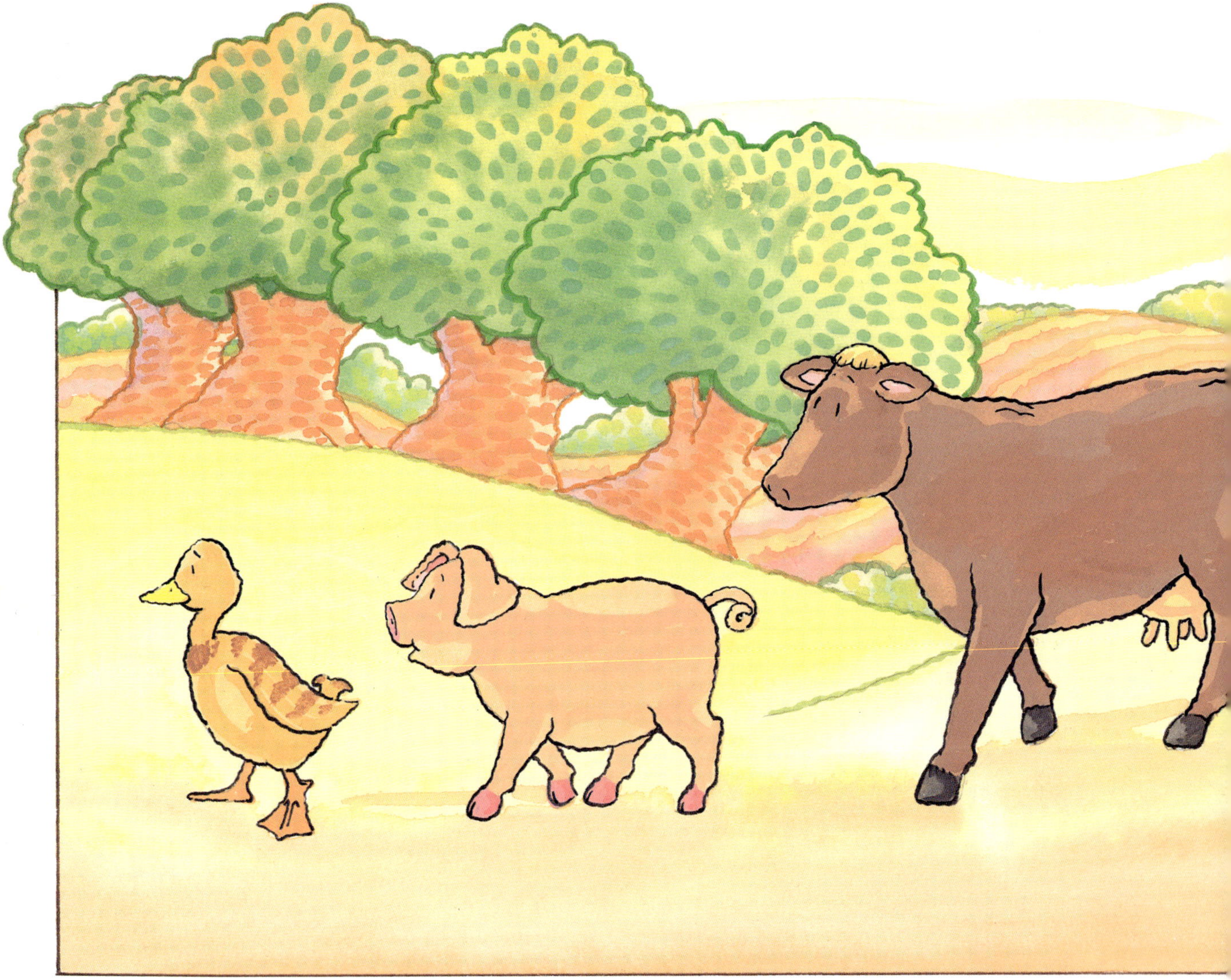

The duck is first.

The cat is last.

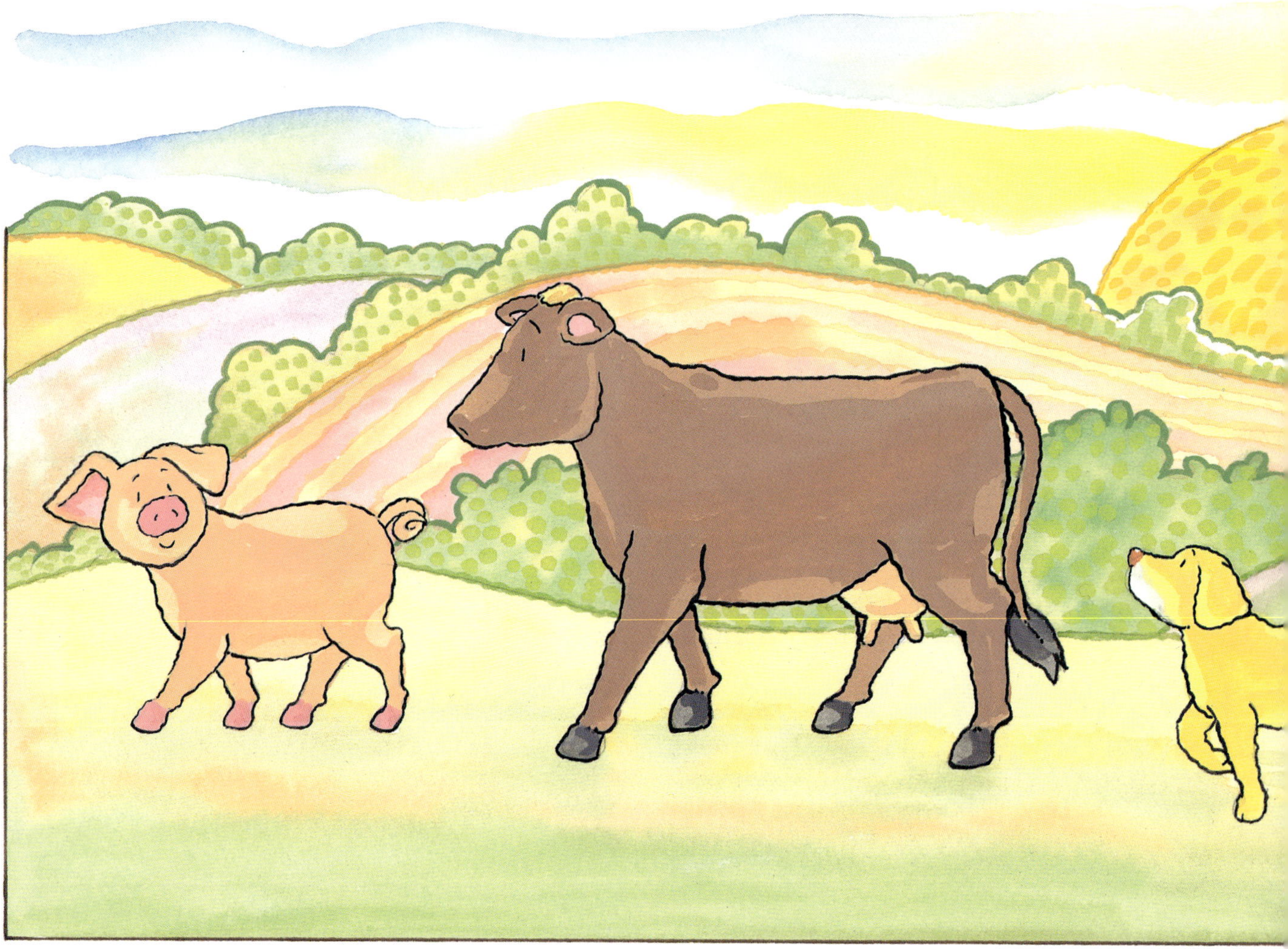

The pig is first.

The duck is last.

6

The cow is first.

The pig is last.

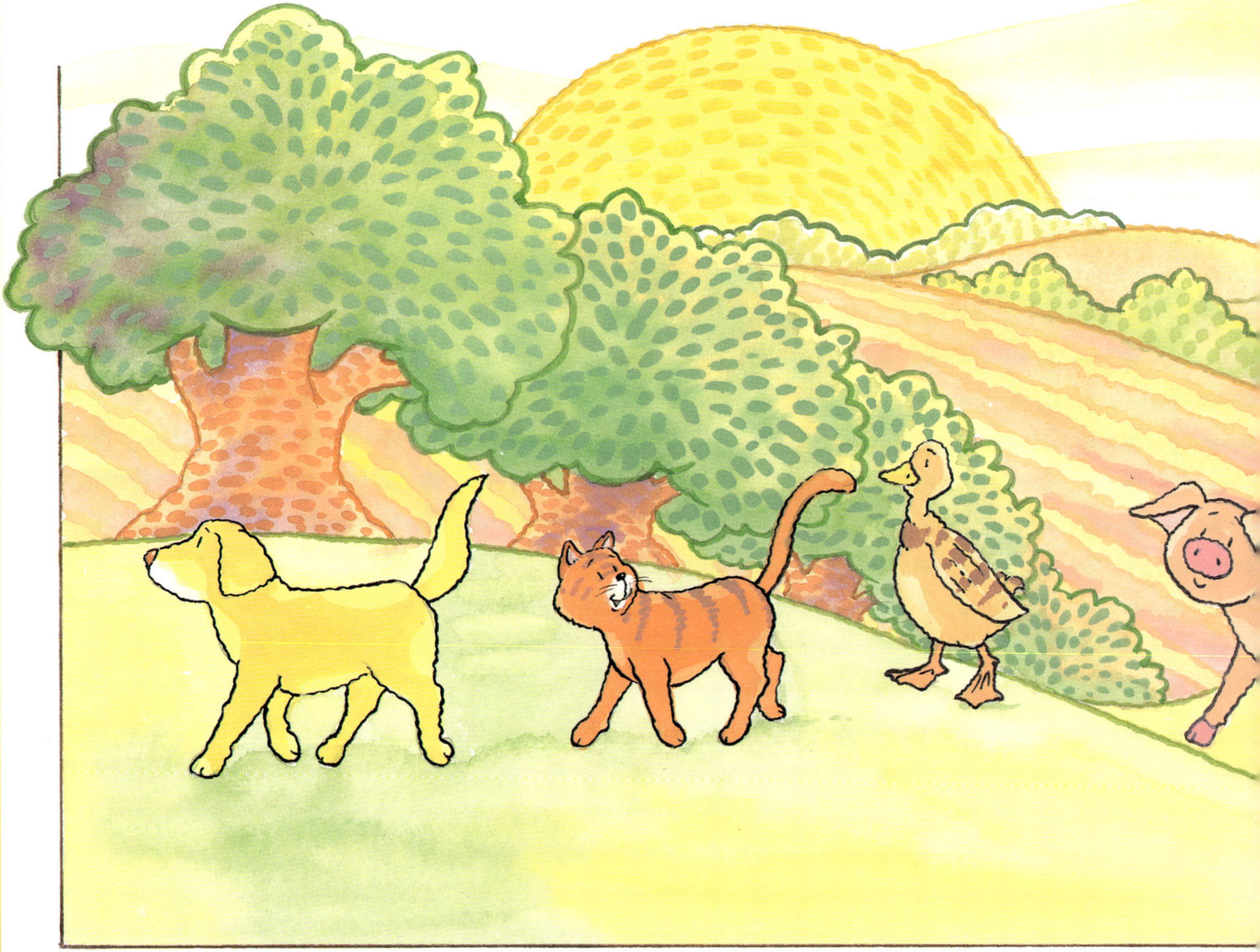

The dog is first.

The cow is last.

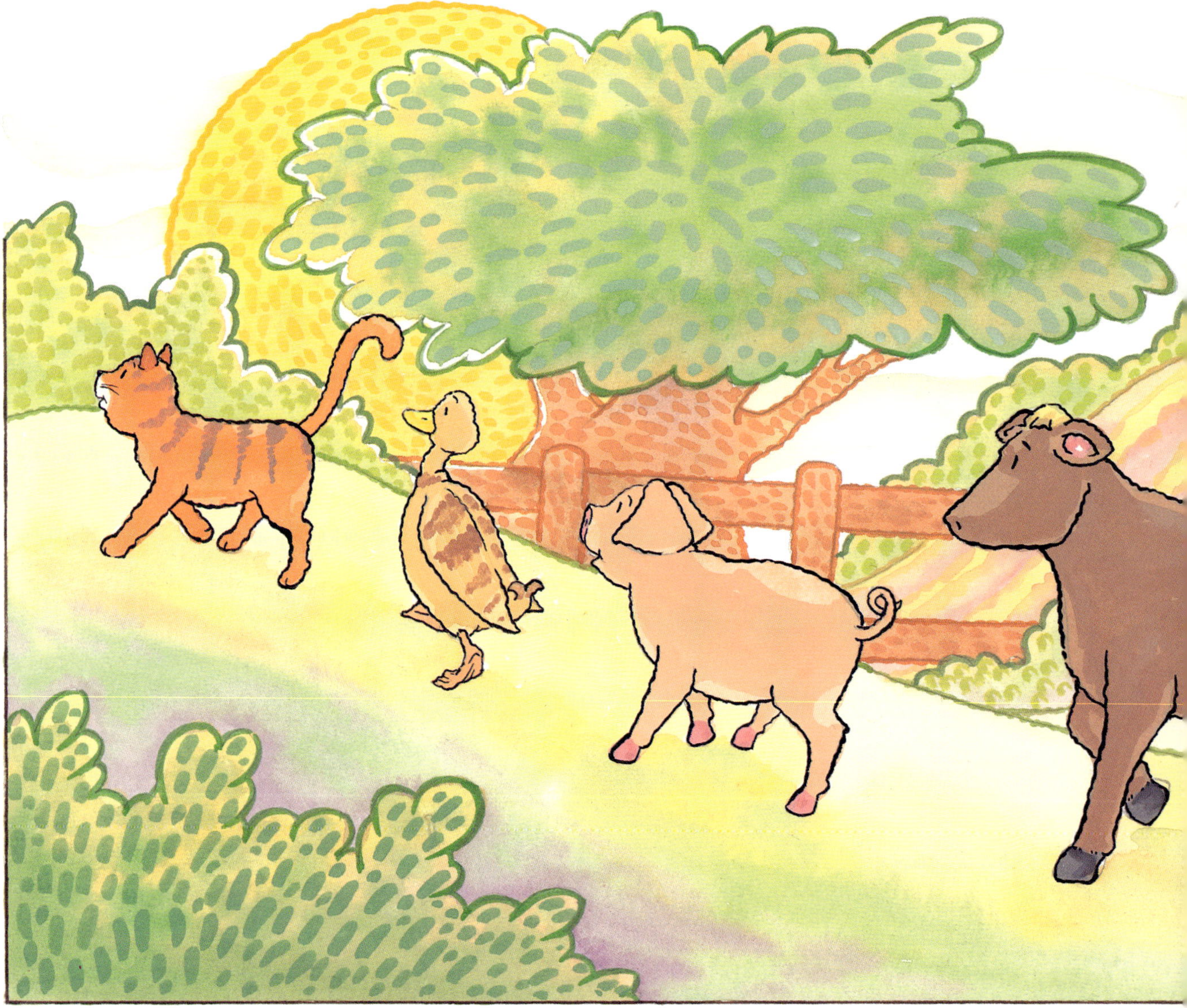

The cat is first.

The dog is last.

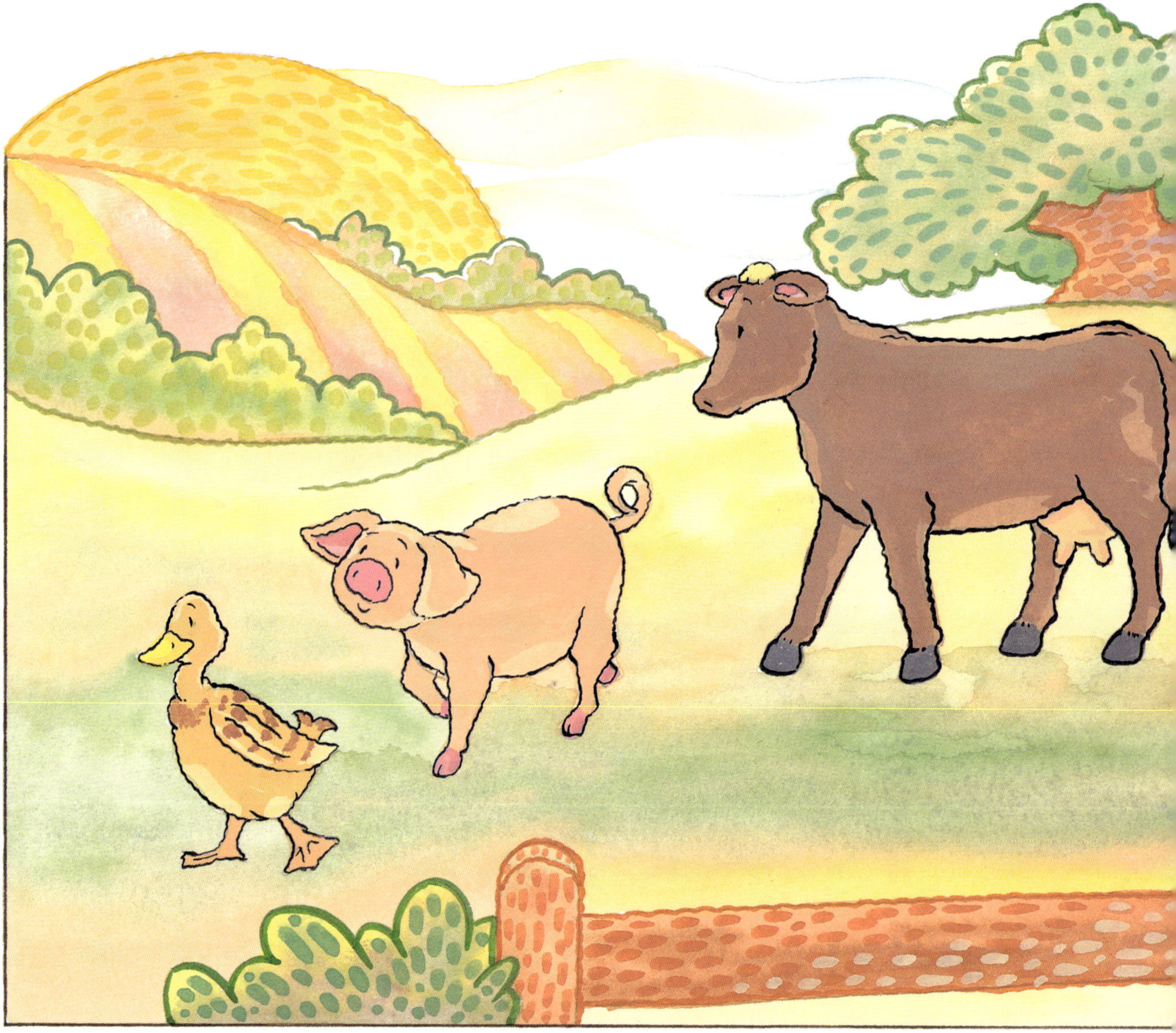

Now who is first?

About the Author

Donna Chicca is a Reading Recovery™ teacher at Frank West School in Bakersfield, California. She has been teaching for seven years. Donna earned both her B.A. and her M.Ed. at California State University, Bakersfield, where she was selected as the outstanding student in the Child Development Program and the Early Child Education Program. She lives in Bakersfield with her supportive husband, Chris, and their three children, Candice, Caleb, and Christopher. In addition to teaching, she is active in her church, and she enjoys being a homemaker.

The development of the *Teacher's Choice Series* was supported by the Reading Recovery project at California State University, San Bernardino. All authors' royalties from the sale of the *Teacher's Choice Series* will be used to support various Reading Recovery projects.

Publisher: Raymond Yuen
Series Editor: Stanley L. Swartz
Editorial Assistant: Bob Rowland
Illustrator: Andrew Geeson
Cover Designer: Steve Morris
Page Designer: Pamela S. Pettigrew

Copyright © 1997 Dominie Press, Inc. All rights reserved. No part of this publication may be reproduced or transmitted in any form or by any means without permission in writing from the publisher. Reproduction of any part of this book, through photocopy, recording, or any electronic or mechanical retrieval system, without the written permission of the publisher is an infringement of the copyright law.

Published by:

Dominie Press, Inc.

1949 Kellogg Avenue
Carlsbad, California 92008 USA

ISBN 1-56270-840-6
Printed in Singapore by PH Productions.
1 2 3 4 5 6 PH 99 98 97